You F*cking Liar

Paul Easton

Published by Paul Easton, 2024.

While every precaution has been taken in the preparation of this book, the publisher assumes no responsibility for errors or omissions, or for damages resulting from the use of the information contained herein.

YOU F*CKING LIAR

First edition. June 29, 2024.

Copyright © 2024 Paul Easton.

ISBN: 979-8991050500

Written by Paul Easton.

Table of Contents

Preface 1
Mask Off 4
Are you happy? 5
My Truest Sentence 7
Liar 8
Your Beautiful Mind 10
Off his meds again... 11
Anxiety 13
Run 14
Still Searching 15
Do you still ache 17
I Hate Hating You 18
Remember me 19
Is it too Late? 21
Orange 22
Honey Bee 24
New York 25
The Shards of Love 26
Naked 27
Forgive? 28
No. I don't love you 30
Anna 32
Only a Decade 33
Scob 35
Together 37
Forever She Said 39
Unfiltered 40
WV 41
Who We Hold Close 43

There Was a Time 45
How to be Happy..46
Toughness 49

Dedicated to all the brave souls who fight internal battles every bright day and every dark night.

Anger and depression are the taste on your lips but kindness and calm will wash it away.

Exhausted but stronger than you know.

I love you.

Paul

Preface

My name is Paul Easton and I am pleased to bring to you my second book "You F*cking Liar" in the poetry series "Thoughts of Scob".

My first book "Thoughts of Scob; I want to make you feel" was the beginning of my dance with writing. After years of trying to navigate my spectrum of emotions from the depths of depression, pain, and anger to the heights of happiness, joy, and love; I felt vulnerable but strong enough to share my unfiltered thoughts and feelings with you.

In this new book, I dive deeper into the human experience of thought, feeling, and emotion from the devastation of heartbreak to what truly makes us feel alive in this world.

I also write about mental health and the challenges and pain we can all face, whether we are going through a crisis ourselves or we are the ones supporting, confused, and picking up the pieces. This subject is one close to my heart.

The main focus of this dance however is for you to discover who you really are. Not who you think you are or who you think you need to be for others, but who you really are when everything has been stripped down and you are completely vulnerable. I want you to take off your mask and be truly honest with yourself.

My hope is that I can provide you with vulnerability and brutal honesty of my own so that you can begin your process of learning who you really are, what you don't need anymore, and what makes you feel alive.

It's not an easy thing to do, but you know it must be done and you have probably known for quite some time.
I want you to stop f*cking lying to yourself.
I hope you enjoy.
Cheers,
Paul

The Truth Behind Your Mask

Mask Off

I want to feel new,
Can I rip the mask off?
Will I be exposed?
Or will I be free?
Free from pretending to be the person I think you want me to be.

   - Paul Easton

Are you happy?

I mean, mask off, are you really happy?

I don't feel okay,
It's different this time,
It's 3am and my thoughts racing,
Guilt as my shadow,
I'm pacing the floor,
Writing on the bathroom mirror again.

Blade pressed to my skin,
Ruminating thoughts,
So heavy so sped up,
But it feels like I'm floating.
They just won't stop,
I'm in pain,
A pain they cannot see,
Would they miss me?
Perceptions of my reality,
What would they say?
Will a slit of the wrist make me feel?
Feel anything other than this.

I feel lonely,
Do you feel like talking?

I want to slide my mask down just a little,
Say what I really feel.
In fact, I want to rip the mask right off,
Say who I really am.

Please know that I'm holding on tightly,
White knuckles,
Eyes closed,
This part of the ride will be over soon,
I won't enjoy it.
Don't worry,
I will get through it,
No matter where I am going.

    - Paul Easton

My Truest Sentence

Truth is I feel so fragile,
I find ways to avoid feeling happy,
Because I know so well the crippling feeling when it ends,
It becomes harder each time to pull myself up from the floor,
So instead, I choose to control my unhappiness,
Looking for the flaws in people,
Detecting the holes in their words,
I seek safety in misery,
I'm sorry.

- Paul Easton

Liar

I'm never truly honest,
Well that's because I'm scared to death,
Scared that you will see through the image I have created of myself for you.

I became who I wanted you to see,
The real me exists behind the mask I reserve for you,
Terrified of being exposed,
I lie not to lose you.

    - Paul Easton

Who Is Your Mind?

Your Beautiful Mind

When you feel that emptiness,
When you feel all alone,
The weight heavy,
Everything just wrong,
When you have stopped being kind to you,
THIS is when you must know...

Your beautiful mind is lying to you.

    - Paul Easton

Off his meds again...

But why?
He was doing so well...

He never wanted this,
Mind murky,
Never trusting,
Thoughts unsettled.

Reluctant he picked his poison,
To free him from his pain.
Wanting better,
For those around him,
Those like you.

Clouds of the mind disappeared,
Feeling so powerful,
Seeing so clear,
He would sleep now,
He was unstoppable,
His Superpower.

The high would wear off,

Becoming stable,
He no longer needed a cure,
"They don't know me" he smirked,
Credibly convinced,
Confidently fine,
He cast aside the chalky white circles.

Wouldn't be long,
Mania rushed in,
Excited, sped up, reckless, and scared,
The hurt would hurt,
All came crashing down.
Now so low,
He tasted defeat,
Feeling weak and ashamed,
Cloudy and murky again.

He needed you, the medicine, anything,
Anything but him.

Tell him he's not alone.

    - Paul Easton

Anxiety

I don't fear what's already here,
I only fear what may come.

- Paul Easton

Run

Where is the place you scream?
Where do you let it all out?
Is it where you hide your flaws?
Tears run down your face,
As you scream into the wall,
Legs weak,
Body warm,
Everything melting,
You want to run,
But don't know where.

- Paul Easton

Still Searching

Searching for feeling,
Grasping for meaning,
Protecting the pain,
Praying for rain,
I'm weary now,
Help me let go.

- Paul Easton

Fuck Love

Do you still ache...

I'm a man so gentle,
I'm soft where others are hard,
I give where others take,
I'm a place you can safely land,
But please don't wrong me.

Please don't.

For its then I become no gentle man,
I will tear you down,
My tongue destroying you,
Over and over again,
Until you feel my hurt,
And we both ache from all that we gave.

    - Paul Easton

I Hate Hating You

I kissed her soft lips sucking in her air,
Desperately trying to inhale her one last time.

It wasn't until she walked away,
That I realized she had cut me.

I looked down at my hands bloody,
My heart still beating,
Close to greeting',
I smiled slowly,
Realizing she had left me one more piece of her.

   - Paul Easton

Remember me

Remember me as the one who loved you the hardest,
Remember me as the one who would fight for and against,
Remember me as the one who made you feel the safest,
Remember me as the one who made you laugh so hard you had to cross your legs,
Remember me as the one who made you smile cheek to cheek,
Illuminating the darkness that had made me.

I remember you,
How you made me feel,
Like I was the only one in the world,
How you moved,
So wild and free,
Brush your bangs from your eyes one last time,
Let them take my soul.

How special was I?
How special were you?
We...

Now I just remember me remembering you,
Hoping you remembering me.

- Paul Easton

Is it too Late?

Listen now,
Silence thoughts,
Forget what you will say next,
Hear her.

She's telling you,
She always has,
With every move she makes,
With every word she doesn't speak,
Hear her now,
Before it's too late.

- Paul Easton

Orange

I stood there bare,
You said not a word,
You closed your eyes,
I didn't see it coming,
You gently ripped my heart from my chest.
I gasped,
But not for air.
Were your big brown eyes laughing or crying?
I couldn't tell.
I felt the gaping hole,
My eyes now as big as yours,
I couldn't believe what I was seeing,
This heart was your home.

I fell to my knees,
Grasping at nothing,
I took back my time,
My love,
My laughs,
The things I only did with you.

It did nothing,

You didn't care,
Said you did,
But you knew you held what mattered.
I hate love,
But not as much as I hate you.

    - Paul Easton

Honey Bee

Lies drip from your warm mouth,
Slow like honey,
Teeth stained from deceit,
Yet you smile with ease.

Grab me with those eyes,
Believe you are giving nothing away,
Locking me in and up,
Making sure I swallow every drop.

Remove your sting honey bee,
Be cruel to be kind,
But you won't,
Because that means losing you in me.

- Paul Easton

New York

Remember when I said I would always be there...
I wish I was.
Still by your side.

- Paul Easton

The Shards of Love

They broke your heart,
Smashed it to smithereens,
Wondering why,
You watched helpless without screaming a word.

They cut you so clean,
You didn't realize you were bleeding until after they were gone,
Piece by piece,
Slice by slice.

Love isn't fair,
And they don't care.
Hands stained red as you pick up the shards of your broken heart,
Knowing now the monster you need to become.

- Paul Easton

Naked

How can I make you feel me?
Really feel me,
Feel this hurt,
Taste this pain,
I'm screaming in silence.
This soul won't sleep,
I lost you,
Now I'm losing me,

Nothing tastes the same without you,
Your naked body lying next to mine,
Singing before the birds each morning,
I still see you smile,
You the great pretender,
Me laying bare.

    - Paul Easton

Forgive?

You say you want this,
You even show me your tears,
I watch them fall,
But then quickly catch myself before I do.

How bad do you want it?
I don't see it pouring out of you,
Fuck those tears,
Your eyes won't convince me now.

Will you scrap for this?
Will you break down the door to get in?
I see you knocking,
Should I let you back in?
It's hard to throw away what we thought was meant to be.

- Paul Easton

Love

No. I don't love you

Little girl with eyes wide open,
One that knows best,
You don't listen to anyone,
Certainly, aren't like the rest.

Through broken doors,
I lost sleep,
Sneaking out,
Your letters cut deep.

Little lady,
You show them all,
Strength, love, and kindness,
How smart you are.
Oh, I wish you could see,
You are not like the rest.
Doubt smothers your restless thoughts,
Perfection plagues your worried soul.
You're exhausted,
One day you'll stop running,
Hopefully from yourself,
It's then that you will love you,

At least just a little.

- Dad

Anna

You wanted my green eyes,
No such luck.
I'm glad,
No green,
But you have what's underneath.

Fits of rage,
Piercing words,
A tongue of two sides,
Make them feel like heaven,
Make them feel like hell.

I love you so much,
Genius that you are.
Take the keys,
I'm showing you the way,
So, you can go far.

   - Dad

Only a Decade

I watch you when you smile,
How could I not?
I smile in return without thought,
I'm never without thought.

I watch others watch you smile,
How could they not?
You carry on,
Your eyes speaking only to mine.

I can't imagine your darkest days,
You could light up the night sky you know,
I can't imagine you drowning in pain filled tears,
You glide with such ease,
Heels barely hitting the floor.
I can't imagine you ever doubting yourself,
But that pale scar on your wrist looks back at me.

I want to ask,
I want to heal,
I want to promise,
But I won't,

I will sing into your soul,
Until you can hear nothing else
My love

    - Paul Easton

Scob

I've been writing for me...
To then serve to you,
Eagerly awaiting your thoughts,
Ready to read your reaction,
To tell me what was wrong,
What was too much,
...always too much.
Dependent on your validation,
I creep back behind the mask I wear so well.
"So, what do you think?"

The phone fell silent,
I took it from my warm cheek to see if he was still there.
"The blood your pen bleeds is yours" he said softly.
So much conviction in his retort,
"You said you wanted to make us feel,
I don't think you ever did.
I think you've been trying to make yourself feel"

Now it was me that fell to silence,
"Write son" he said
"Just write. Doesn't matter what they think,

Let it pour out of you,
You only get to do it once.
Stop trying to control how, when, and to who,
People will take from it what they need"

I exhaled,
Feeling now bold,
"Thanks Dad" I said.
"Alright son, gotta go talk to you soon"

    - Paul Easton

Together

Oh, it's not where you go,
You can brag all you like,
But deep down you know,
It's who comes with you.
I've laughed places with you,
Where I've cried with others.

- Paul Easton

How to be Happy

by Paul Easton

I don't know...

Forever She Said

Hurry...
We are wasting time not being together,
Another night apart,
I want you,
Another meal on our own,
I need you,
"Relax babe we have forever" she smiled and said
I frowned, paused, then swallowed,
Trying not to panic...

"How long is forever?" I asked
She laughed with teeth as white as pearls,
"A long-time babe" she said playfully, Shaking her head,
I couldn't laugh back,
I didn't want to,
Because I know how long forever is,
White Rabbit once told Alice
"Sometimes, just one second"

- Paul Easton

Unfiltered

"Poetry is art" she said
"But I'm worried how it will come across" I told her,
Looking at me detached she said sharply "Art's not filtered"
I nodded in agreement, not to her words but to feeling her passion,
Fuck, she was stunning.

Uncomfortable in the silence I spoke up,
"What if they don't understand what I'm trying to say?"
"Poetry is yours" she said softly without looking up,
"It doesn't need to be explained Paul"
She rarely used my name.

I wanted everything that she was.

    - Paul Easton

WV

500 miles they said to walk,
Just to be the man to be with you.
Days into my attempt,
The sweltering summer heat had me beat,
I'm no further along this Appalachian trail.

Tennessee, Maryland, Virginia…
Where I was? I had no idea,
Sugar maple surrounding me,
I think I heard a roar.

There it stood swallowing up my path,
A great black bear.
Then a noise so loud I fell to the ground,
The bear disappeared as quickly as it appeared,
He looked down at me extending his hand.

Rugged as the mountains around us,
In his tanned smooth buckskin,
He led me down a holler,
Rifle in hand,
A kindness in his eyes.

We reached the hilltop,
My eyes open wide,
Almost heaven,
The natural beauty of this mountain state,
He passed me his flask,
Moonshine... I smiled.
"Where am I" I asked,
"Kanawha" he said.

A place where mountaineers are always free,
Land of Pinky,
Country roads,
Take me home,
West Virginia.

    - Paul Easton

Who We Hold Close

You are so quick to say hurtful things to those you care for,
A spouse, significant other, child, parent, sibling,
Rarely does your sharp tongue mean these words.
What sense would it make?
We love these people.

The tighter you hold them,
They see more of your vulnerabilities,
Some you have never exposed,
Showing the holes that you possess,
Revealing what's behind your mask.

It's harder to say sorry,
To say what you really mean,
Fearing you may be left bare,
Damage you may never recover from.

You ask for their all,
But you can't give your all to them.
The person whose soul you want to touch most,
You destroy with ease.

Ah... deep breath,
Relax your face,
Listen a little more,
Tame your wild tongue,
Listen a little more,
Meet fear face to face,
Look it head to toe,
Step back,
Give fear its fatal blow,
Trust.

Trust you,
So, you can trust who you love.

    - Paul Easton

There Was a Time

Remember the good old days?
When everything felt free and fun,
Time didn't limit your happiness,
Money didn't factor your joy,
And you weren't focused on impressing anyone...

Me too.

    - Scob

How to be Happy

(Okay, so I'll take a stab in the dark)
What makes you happy?
What sings to your soul?
You already know what makes it cry,
So why do you act as if you don't know?

Well...
I think you have always known,
But you are caught in a haze of doubt,
Weighed down and terrified to change.

Happiness is not a person,
Not even the one you still long for.
It's not a job title,
It's not money.

It's a feeling,
It's freedom of choice knowing you can make the best of any result,
It's being completely enthralled in each moment,
It's knowing that you aren't afraid to be who you really are,
No matter who disagrees or leaves.

Happiness is knowing that you won't always feel happy,
But also knowing that the sad times won't last.

Happiness is dancing in the winds of change...

Shed all that distracts and weighs you down,
If you can't, discover a way to make it play,
Resist change no longer,
No matter how hard and painful,
Swim with the stream,
Never against,
You will find what is meant for you.

Happiness is dancing in the winds of change with your eyes closed trusting your every move as you feel the music enter your soul.

- Paul Easton

BONUS

Toughness

I'm not a tough man, but I'm certainly not a soft man. I never look for a fight, but when challenged I rarely back down. Oh, and I hate bullies, in any form.

"He got it from his mama" the saying goes. Well, I certainly got it from my mama. Let me tell you how...

I was 11 years old back in Scotland, it was the school summer holidays. The Scottish sun was scorching... just joking, I wanted to make sure you were paying attention. The Scottish sun never scorches, hence my perfectly pale complexion. My friend Mike and I were hanging out playing outside his house. In the distance and along the long narrow street that ran towards Mike's house, we saw Jake.

Jake MacMillan... oh, Jake fucking MacMillan... the neighborhood bully. Trouble was an understatement. Usually I had sympathy for those tormented souls but I had zero for Jake. Zero.

Mike nodded to me, I turned and clocked Jake pacing towards us... **"shit"** I said as I quickly dug into my pockets but I could feel

Jake's laser focused eyes on my hands as he got closer, so I spoke to Mike like everything was normal.

Jake approached us with his usual bloated confident swag, you see Jake was one of those guys that was too dumb to be scared of anything, his parents were drunks, and his older brother was already in prison. Jake was in the same grade as Mike and I but he was 2 years older, I will let you do the math on that one, lord knows Jake couldn't.

Now almost face to face Jake looked at Mike and said **"how much money you got on you?"** Mike said **"none"** looking towards his house praying one of his parents would come out and intervene the stick up. Jake turned to me and said **"how much money you got on you Easton?"** I said **"I got nothing Jake, honest"**. Of course, I was lying, I had a whopping 65 pence in change after spending 1 pound and 35 pence at the corner shop on candy. Jake then deployed his usual tactic **"alright fuckers, jump up and down"**. This was Jake's method, back then in the early 90's change was a thing. He would make his victims jump up and down with their hands on their head so he could hear any change jingle in their pockets. Come to think of it now, Jake's bandit entrepreneurship handsfree technique wasn't too shabby. Now you might be thinking, ok so what? he takes your change big deal… well, a couple of things… one, your change you got from the corner shop was a big thing back then and two, if you had lied to Jake he would not only take your change he beat your ass for lying…. And they say there is no honor amongst thieves.

I rarely had change in my pockets. I either spent it all at once or I was always running and jumping so it would get in the way and fall out.

Well I knew what was coming next. As I jumped praying the change wouldn't touch each other in my pocket; it did. His eyes lit up and he got right in my face… I can still see his beady eyes and the zits on his cheeks. He said **"cough it up Easton"**. I had no alternative, I glanced at Mike who gave me a faint-hearted smile to say sorry buddy. I am surprised he didn't run into his house and leave me, but as much as he might have considered the idea he stood with me, his friend.

Jake punched me square in the nose and then pushed me onto the grass. I could taste the blood. I was ready to defend the next blow, maybe a kick? Maybe a flying punch? but nothing. Jake began to laugh, to be honest I didn't think he was capable of such emotion. As I looked up at him, puzzled, he pointed to my shoulder. I had landed right in Mike's massive dogs' shit. I was now penniless, bloodied, stinking of dog shit, and mortified. I did what any 11-year-old would do… I ran home.

Home was only 3 minutes away. I ran up the concrete steps to the front door, trying to outrun the smell of warm dog shit on my shoulder. I tried the door handle but it was locked. My house was never locked, never. My mum opened the big living room window which looked to the door and out into the street. She was proud because the council had recently fitted the houses of the street with double glazing. She had been cleaning them from the inside. She looked at me confused and asked me what was going on. I said **"mum, mum, open the door, open the door"**. Unphased, she looked me up and down pausing her curious gaze at my bloody nose and the shit on my shoulder. She said softly **"who did this to you?"**, I told her that I fell (note: why does every kid ever say this?). She then began to get angry, she said not so softly **"who did this to you Paul?"**. I told her that it was Jake. She asked why and where. I was impatient and wanted inside badly. She cared not. She paused and looked at me again, still from inside the window frame now open wide and said very slowly **"You are going to go back over there and you are going to skelp Jakes arse or you will never get back in this house"** (to "skelp" someone's arse in Scottish means to kick someone's ass). I was now horrified. My mother, my own mother, flesh and blood was not only not protecting me from the bully but she was adding extra pressure and a threat!

I said **"fine then"**, turned and headed back to Mike's, but my super intelligent 11-year-old, nearly 12-year-old brain was operating at full cylinder, so I decided to hide around the corner so my mum wouldn't see me. After 10 minutes (it was probably only 2 minutes in reality) I went back to my house and sheepishly said" okay **mum I did it, I kicked his arse"**. This time she didn't even play the game, she said **"Paul if you don't kick his arse right now I'm going to kick YOUR arse"**.

Now let me pause here. My mother is the most determined, strongest, and bravest human being I know. I know we are supposed to say that about our parents, but I mean that shit. She is bold like a lion and her kindness to those that need it is relentless. However, make no mistake about this; I am more scared of my mother than I am any other person on this planet, especially at 11 years old. No disrespect dad.

Jake never stood a chance. I didn't respond to my mum, I turned and walked back to Mike's house, that 3-minute journey felt like 10 seconds. They were still there, Jake probably not letting Mike go, maybe you could say Jake was looking for a friend and was just misguided. I didn't give a fuck. I could smell the fresh shit on my shoulder as I walked up to him, I landed a right hook on his cheek, then another, then another, he fell over, I sat on him and punched him left and right until Mike's dad magically appeared and pulled me off him. I took off my shirt and threw it in Jake's face.

I walked home, this time it did feel like 3 minutes, I never once looked over my shoulder as I knew Jake wouldn't be back. I walked up the concrete stairs, this time smelling no shit, my mum looked at me and then opened the door. We never said a word about it that day, that night, or ever.

I didn't see Jake around much for the rest of the school summer holidays, but when I did he would cross the street, literally and would look down at the ground. I wasn't proud of what I did, but I didn't regret it either. It was like I had blacked out and became this 11-year-old Mike Tyson. When I saw him at school that semester we avoided each other. Jake sadly didn't last long at our school as he was moved out to a school for troubled youths a few months later.

I don't hate Jake. Looking back, I feel sorry for him now, because he was dealt a shitty hand in life, but at the time his lashing out and abusive behavior affected me directly so it was difficult for me to be compassionate and see anything but hate in that moment. I think this is true for all of us when it comes to situations that directly affect us, we struggle to recognize why the other person is acting the way they are towards us. That makes it extremely difficult to show kindness or compassion in that moment. It is hard to detach ourselves or zoom out and take the view from above to see that that person may be the one that is really suffering.

I strongly believe that most parents do the best they know how when they know how with their children, shit remember they are just figuring out life as they go also. "Top Ten 10 Parenting Tips for Boys" Get the fuck out of here. Those click bait articles are egotistical vomit. Yes, there are common similarities and best practices in parenting but remember there are so many internal and external factors that can shape a child and a family. Parents... keep pushing, figuring shit out best you can, enforcing accountability, caring, listening, talking, yelling, apologizing, loving, crying, laughing. It's an experience and all you can do is the best you know how when you know how.

My mother gave me the gift of teaching me how to stand up for myself by myself. I am sure it wasn't easy for her to watch and take that gamble, maybe Jake would have given me a second skelping or maybe she knew I was a mini Mike Tyson, either way I don't believe that was her goal. Her goal was teaching me to never back down from a bully, to stand up for what is right, and to create courage by learning to forget fear, even for just 3 minutes.

Thank you, mum. I love you.
Paul

About the Author

Paul Easton hails from Dunfermline, Scotland, United Kingdom, the birth place of Andrew Carnegie. He moved to Virginia, USA in 2005 to follow his dream of coaching basketball. Paul served as an assistant high school coach, head high school coach, and as a basketball trainer for all ages for 19 years. Paul references the meaningful relationships and deep connections he has been fortunate to build along the way as his favorite part of coaching.

Paul worked many jobs to make the dream of coaching a reality from kitchen worker to security guard to Director of security, and many other interesting odd jobs along the way!

It was in November, 2023 that he decided to put pen to paper or fingers to keyboard to be more accurate and started to write his unfiltered thoughts of his own life experiences. Paul explains that the more he wrote the braver he became in expressing his vulnerabilities and fears. His aim is to help others who experience similar feelings and emotions. His form of poetry and story telling became his most fluid way of expressing his raw feelings and emotions.

When he is not writing ferociously into his phones notes section everywhere from the wee hours of the morning to stuck in standstill traffic, Paul loves playing and watching football (soccer), Manchester United diehard, getting lost in song lyrics, traveling back to Scotland to see is family, and spending time with his two children. Oh, he also has a black cat...

Read more at www.thoughtsofscob.com.

www.ingramcontent.com/pod-product-compliance
Lightning Source LLC
Chambersburg PA
CBHW060219050426
42446CB00013B/3111